Winning the Digital Gamble

5 Disruption Levers to Jump Start Your Enterprises' Relevancy in the Fourth Industrial Revolution

Raheel Retiwalla and Randhir Kalsi

Winning the Digital Gamble

Printed by:
Raheel Retiwalla

Published in the United States of America

ISBN-13: 978-1543286458
ISBN-10: 1543286453

Here's What's Inside...

Introduction 1

CHAPTER 1: Digital Disruption
Opportunity with Smart Services 5

CHAPTER 2: The 5 Disruption Levers 23

CHAPTER 3: The Digital Culture 29

CHAPTER 4: The Digital Leader 32

CHAPTER 5: The Customer Experience 38

CHAPTER 6: The Operating
Model Strategy 42

CHAPTER 7: Hardware, Data
and the Cloud... 60

Chapter 8: The Execution 74

Chapter 9 - Choosing Your Partners..................... 80

Summary 84

Introduction

The Fourth Industrial Revolution is upon us. In fact, "Mastering the Fourth Industrial Revolution" was the theme of the World Economic Forum Annual Meeting 2016 in Davos-Klosters, Switzerland. The Fourth Industrial Revolution represents brand new opportunities for enterprises to imagine ways in which technology embedded in their current or new product or service permeates and drastically improves society.

Many times, it is difficult to realize one is in the midst of a revolution or a revolution even exists when the revolution is in its infancy which is the case here. We have had the honor of working with many clients who have seized this opportunity deciding to disrupt themselves, their industries, their business models and who they consider as a customer. The disruption path enterprises take is not easy. Figuring out the impact of the disruption and charting a course to transform has been difficult for most.

The questions we usually get from clients are more commonly around "How do we get started?" or "How should we think about the opportunity?" or "We are a hardware company and do not understand the cloud or software" or "What kind of an organizational structure do we need to make this successful?". Very few if any have said "We don't think this applies to us". In this book, we have modelled what has worked into a framework for managing this digital disruption. The framework is based on the various experiences each of us has had individually and as a team working for and with many enterprises. We have felt the sense of urgency that leaders are facing and have responded as such with this book that we hope you can digest easily to design your own digital launchpad.

We're highly energized by the impact digital disruption has on both the people creating the transformation and customers and their experience with the organization.

Because of advancements in technology and things like the cloud and advanced analytics, companies can quickly start to see success with their own digital transformation. It no longer takes years to see success. Now you can start to see results in months, possibly even weeks.

This revolution is seeing a blurring of what is business and what is technology like never before. Not only does this apply to the company operations but also disruptive to employees many of whom will need to re-tool and re-train to complete the new capabilities a leader will need in this digital age. Companies in the retail and auto industries—and many others—are becoming technology companies, and technology companies, in some cases, are becoming industry leaders, as in retail. The frontier is ahead of you, and there are huge opportunities to influence the future of your organization and your customers in a positive way.

An added and often overlooked bonus is that you can have so much fun doing this type of work. It requires a lot of creativity to do a digital transformation right, and that is one of the reasons we wanted to write this book. We want more companies to create their own successful digital transformations—but with, the odds stacked heavily in their favor.

Enjoy the book!

We hope this book educates you on the "do's" and "don'ts" of navigating your company through its own successful digital transformation. We have tried to generalize but clearly each case will have its nuances. We have described the components of the framework at a high level to help you begin the conversation and to help you put your arms around the opportunity. And we hope this book inspires you to have the courage to pursue your ideas with huge amounts of conviction and energy and to know that there are great resources and partners out there with which you can team up in a very low-risk, affordable way.

To Your Winning Digital Transformation!

Raheel Retiwalla &
Randhir Kalsi

CHAPTER 1: Digital Disruption Opportunity with Smart Services

There has been a significant rise in the number of enterprises considering connected products and associated smart services as part of their digital strategies. That is partly due to the hype around the Internet of Things (IoT), partly due to perceived industry disruption, and partly due to the hype around the term "digital transformation." In working with many enterprises and being a part of transformational programs, we can tell you that the Digital Disruption is real and that there is significant value in channeling the disruption and evaluating opportunities with Smart Services. To understand the opportunity, we have to understand what we mean by Digital Disruption and Smart Services.

Digital Disruption is a new conversation with customers that creates significant incremental value for both the customer and for the enterprise offering the service or product. The values that get created for all parties can be measured by two things that need to be viewed and evaluated together. The first is what we call the Customer Experience Quotient (CEQ) and the second are the Customer Engagement Outcomes. Both are defined below:

- Customer Experience Quotient (CEQ) – This is made up of five factors that influence customer experience that can be measured as a quotient:

  1. Self-Service – There are two benefits of enabling self-service for your product or service. First, consumers and customers love to be in control of how and when to interact with a product or service. Second, self-service drives down cost. A great example of self-service is the airline industry, where passengers now reserve their own tickets, check themselves in, select their own seats, and attach their own baggage tags after they check in. A decade ago there were significant costs for airlines to perform these functions, which are now happily being done by passengers. Investing in a digital medium for passengers to perform these functions through digital transformation has served airlines very well. Self-service has benefited the United States Postal Service (USPS) as well. Gone are the days of long lines at the counter. Now customers can use the self-service kiosks to get pretty much all of their postal transactions done.

  2. Convenience – How convenient is this new product or service to the customer? Convenience could mean the product is

easy to use, saves time, or is based on self-service. I don't need to phone a call center because it's what I want, when I want it, how I want it, and in the form I want it in. A great simple example is the app "ParkChicago." Living in Chicago and using the app to pay for parking throughout the city is extremely convenient, so convenient that on a day trip to Lansing, Michigan, the sudden need for quarters to pay at the meter felt out of place.

3. Personalization – The service or product is personalized, which means it's designed for me. It's not general. There are examples of where a digital interaction or engagement with an organization would take into account my personal preferences and what I have bought in the past. We may feel personalization is important because it shows that a company knows and cares about us as customers, is concerned about what we like and don't like, and adapts to us. The best example of this is the way Amazon has personalized every part of the shopping experience.

4. Entertainment – What we are seeing is that that the customer experience is colliding with the entertainment industry.

Consumers want to be entertained whilst they are iterating with a smart service provider. If I am a fitness fanatic and can compare my fitness data with my friend's fitness data, I am entertained while getting fit. People want to be amused and be entertained by the digital economy, while benefitting from it. Take another example of the wildly popular game from Niantic, Pokémon GO, which allows a person to seamlessly go between the "augmented reality" of the digital Pokémon realm and the GPS coordinates of real locations.

5. Predictive Ability and Proactivity – To be predictive and proactive means you're pushing intelligence to me and anticipating my needs, as opposed to waiting for me to tell you. There is a context of intent; you understand my intent as far as predicting is concerned, and that's how you can be more proactive.

- Customer Engagement Outcomes – How are your product and your service influencing customer behavior to achieve the outcomes you have identified both for you as the enterprise, and the customer? Engagement to you as an enterprise could mean a variety of metrics like wallet share, conversion rates, profitability margin, repeat business, etc.

The area of business or customer outcomes is a critical area, as not being clear about these means that you cannot know if they show up. To this end we elaborate on this topic in chapter 6 and discuss 'well formed outcomes'.

To discuss the second concept of Smart Services, we need to first talk about the Internet of Things (IoT). More importantly, let's talk about the "Things" part of the IoT. "Things" in IoT can be defined as a physical object that has all of the following five components:

1. **Embedded electronics**, like a controller board and a microprocessor
2. **Sensors** that measure something and collect data
3. **Actuators** that allow control of that thing
4. **Software** that adds a level of local intelligence to the thing
5. **Network connectivity** that enables these things to connect and transmit their data either to a local network or to the Internet

Let's drive this home with an example —in this case, thermostats—and evaluate which one can be considered an Internet of Things "thing."

	This is a Thing but it is Not an IoT "Thing"	This is a Thing and it is an IoT "Thing"
Embedded Electronics	Yes	Yes
Embedded Sensors	Yes	Yes
Actuators	Yes	Yes
Embedded Software	Maybe	Yes
Network Connectivity	No	Yes

We are often asked, "Can the thing left in its current state become an IoT 'thing'?" The answer is yes. With hardware engineering, any non-IoT "thing" can become an IoT "thing." These are stand-alone "things" that can be engineered to becoming connected. Also, note that a thing can connect to the cloud directly like the Nest thermostat can or through an intermediary like how transport has been connected by Uber or how some health monitoring products connect via an app on the phone.

The question really is: Why would you want to do that? If the IoT is really about the "thing," then what is the real value for the enterprise? The value is in the services that these things can enable and it is these services that truly unlock the potential of the Fourth Industrial Revolution. Let's call them "Smart Services."

At the heart of Smart Services are opportunities enabled by applying **intelligent rules** to the combination of real-time data generated by the sensors on IoT 'things." This data includes historical enterprise data, metadata (customer, product, SKU), and ambient data (weather and traffic). It is the ability to interpret the combination of data by applying these intelligent rules that exhibits the value in the Smart Service. The higher the intelligence and action, the bigger the disruption and higher the returns. The higher degree of interpretation of the data you do versus your customers, the higher the disruption and therefore the returns. A simple example of Uber converting how far is your driver into specific minutes before the driver will show up to pick you up is an example of data interpretation for superior customer experience.

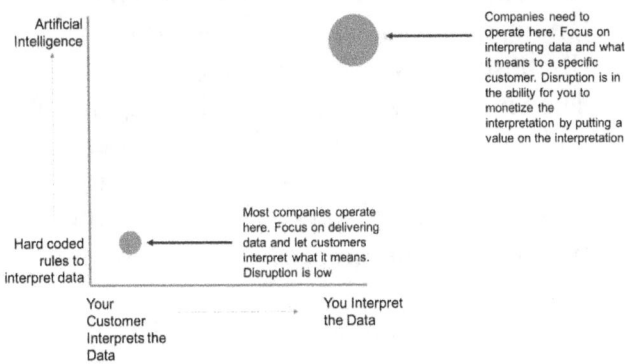

Artificial Intelligence

Hard coded rules to interpret data

Companies need to operate here. Focus on interpreting data and what it means to a specific customer. Disruption is in the ability for you to monetize the interpretation by putting a value on the interpretation

Most companies operate here. Focus on delivering data and let customers interpret what it means. Disruption is low

Your Customer Interprets the Data

You Interpret the Data

Smart Services disrupt traditional business models, drive organic growth, increase net revenue, allow the introduction of subscription-based revenue models, and focus on bringing the concepts of the Customer Engagement Quotient and Customer Engagement alive.

Whether you're a B2B (business-to-business) environment or a B2C (business-to-consumer) environment, achieving digital disruption with Smart Services is relevant and impactful. The B2C environment has clearly seen the joint strategy of launching an IoT "thing" coupled with Smart Services to add significant growth and value to the enterprise.

Let's take a few case studies of B2C companies that have done just this with great success. In each case study, we will discuss:

1. The Company
2. The Thing – For the product to be an IoT "thing," it needs to have the qualities discussed above.
3. The Smart Services that provide significant value to the company and its customers
4. The Disrupted parties – Who or what is being disrupted, either just by the Thing or by the combination of the Thing and the Smart Services.
5. Whether the combination of the Thing and the Smart Services meet the Customer Experience Quotient discussed above
6. Whether the enterprise benefits from the Customer Engagement Outcomes

Case Study 1: Apple and the iPhone

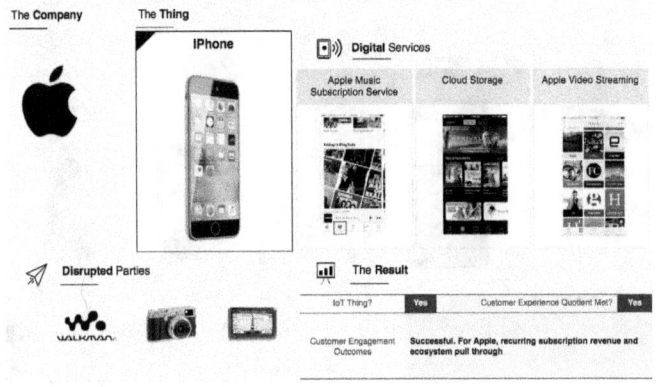

Case Study 2: Eureka Forbes and the Aquaguard

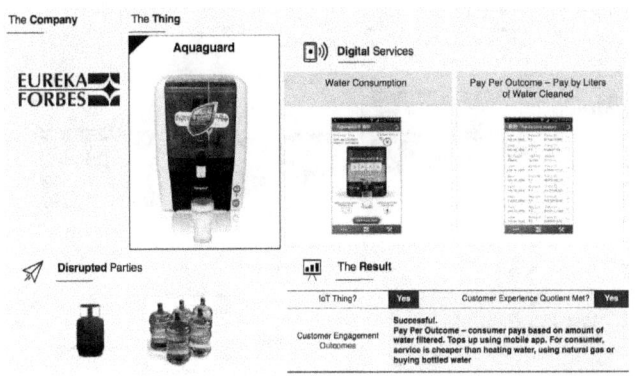

Case Study 3: Samsung and The Family Hub Refrigerator

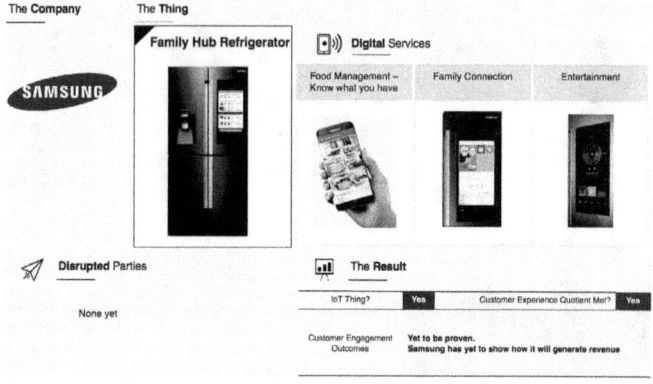

Case Study 4: Amazon and the Amazon Go Store

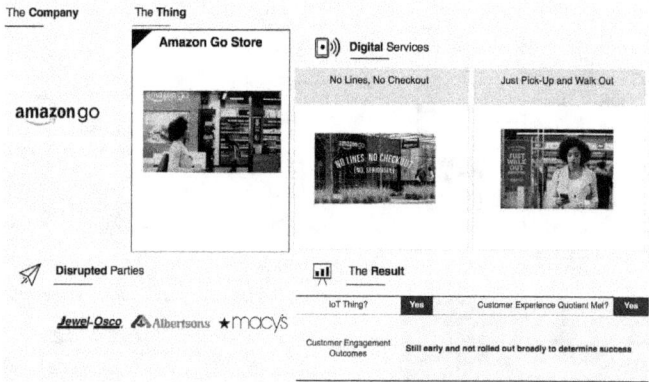

Case Study 5: Redbox

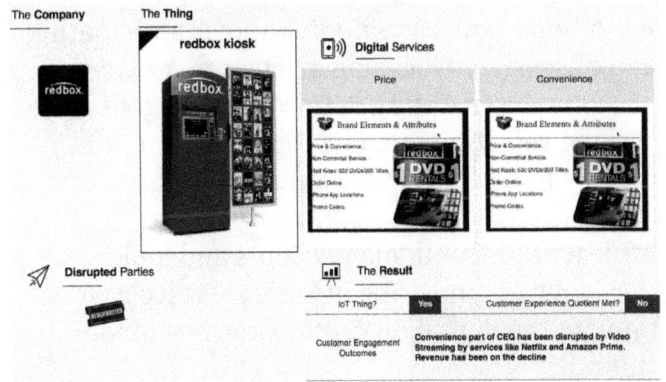

The **Company**

The **Thing**

Disrupted Parties

Digital Services

The Result

IoT Thing?	Yes	Customer Experience Quotient Met?	No

Customer Engagement Outcomes — Convenience part of CEQ has been disrupted by Video Streaming by services like Netflix and Amazon Prime. Revenue has been on the decline

Understanding the Range of Opportunities with Smart Services

As shown in the case studies above, anticipating and obsessively focusing on customer experience based on interpreting data with intelligent rules and the resulting monetization opportunities is the key to disruption via Smart Services.

After working with many clients and looking at the evolving landscape of Smart Services, we think of the digital disruption journey in four stages:

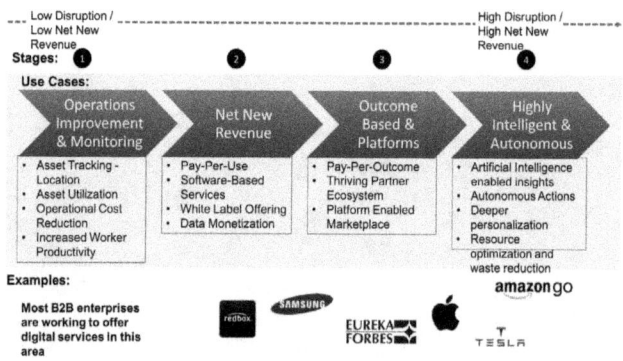

It is not important to follow the stages sequentially or in order. As you can see, Amazon is disrupting with Amazon Go directly at Stage 4 and Eureka Forbes with the Aquaguard took a stand-alone product and converted it to a connected product with par-per-outcomes services – something we suggest as Stage 3. In our experience, B2B enterprises have a hard time looking beyond Use Cases made possible in Stage 1. In particular, many B2B companies and a good portion of B2C companies selling industrial products immediately gravitate toward the low-hanging use cases offered here in Stage 1. Their focus is more on providing data and not as much on the interpretation of data which as we have noted determines the degree of disruption and the resultant profits. There is less thought put into the core concepts described in the book above specific to the Customer Experience Quotient (convenience, predictability and personalization) and Customer Engagement Outcomes. The result is enough excitement to convert stand-alone products into connected products, but not enough of a business case for executives to invest in such a transformation. It is our hope that change agents and digital leaders within an enterprise go outside their comfort zone and think broadly about a new relationship with customers that opens up new business models.

For a transformation to digital disruption caused by Smart Services to occur, many, many areas have to change within an enterprise. Because of that, almost everybody is already out of their comfort zone. Enterprises may have 50%, 60%, or 70% of the capabilities, but they're definitely missing something.

At the heart of it, Digital Disruption is like any other product innovation that's been happening for the last century. Historically, product innovation stats show that more than 95% of product innovations or service innovations fail; they don't meet the goals that are set. If you consider the technology adoption curve (Everett M. Rogers [March 6, 1931 – October 21, 2004] Diffusion of Innovation) and the addition of Chasm Theory (Geoffrey A. Moore), then it's clear that getting your idea to go mainstream is not a new issue.

The difference this time around is that in today's digital economy, the market is a lot less forgiving because of the speed at which change is happening, and the speed at which consumers expect more. Getting across this chasm, which is the theory of getting new products successfully to market, is a whole lot more complicated today because the stakes are high. That is what we refer to as the "digital gamble."

The questions become: Do you tip-toe your way through the disruption, or do you go all the way in? Does your current business fade away? If so, how quickly? What is the first-mover advantage here? We can see that the first-mover advantage pays handsomely, whether the mover is a new digital company like Uber, Airbnb, Fitbit, or Tesla or a traditional industrial B2C product company that decides to engage directly with its end consumers versus previously only selling only through a channel.

Another theory is the idea of the "whole product." The whole product involves thinking about various aspects of the entire product innovation, which not only include hardware engineering, but also take into consideration Cloud, data, operations, and customer experience.

There is confusion about what digital disruption means and what an organization has to do to truly realize its business potential. The main thing to realize is that this is not the time to drag along the legacy, whether it's legacy systems; previous non-depreciated assets; people with legacy mindsets, including leadership; or the traditional business case approval process. The market is moving too fast during this transition to the digital economy to use these traditional process and assets.

Is your innovation continuous or discontinuous? Each of these will result in a very different journey. Stop and ask if the prize is big enough to break all the previous rules? If your innovation is discontinuous and the stakeholders don't see the prize as big enough, then stop.

Calibrate what you are trying to achieve with the transformation and communicate it accordingly.

We have created a transformation hierarchy framework based on complexity, risk, and level of innovation required. Knowing what you're in for is the first step. Only then can you decide how you will organize the 'success holders,' so they all feel they can give their best. We have a hierarchy that we use to think through the sources of energy supply and energy drain, depending upon the type of transformation.

KNOW WHAT YOU'RE IN FOR?	EXTERNAL DISRUPTION	INTERNAL DISRUPTION	EXAMPLES
Real-Time Data for new business models	High	Low*	• Internet of Things (IoT) • Vertical industry alliances for common customers • Fitbit
Disrupt the Industry Value Chains leveraging cloud & mobile	High	Low*	• Uber
Get creative with the Customer Experience	Medium - High	High	• Become transparent with a digital experience • Transaction level tracking
Build Integrated Customer Experience through Journey Mapping	Medium	High	• Integrated marketing, sales and customer services • Omni channel CRM • Field Service integration
Reduce Operating Expenditure - automate back office and middle office processes	Low	Medium	• Billing • Manage my Account • Data Visualization Portal
Reduce Operating Expenditure - supply chain innovation	Low	Low - Medium	• Outsourcing / Offshoring • Supplier Consolidation • Capex to Opex shift
Acquisition / Merger	High	Medium	• GTM integration • CRM and ERP integration
Divesture	High	High	• IT Systems carve out • People decisions while keeping the engine running

Y-axis label: Complexity of Transformation (High at top)

* Boards face a decision whether to leverage existing operations and people and attempt to drive innovation across the organization or do a carve out and create the "safe zone" to allow the freedom for the creativity to occur. This is just a rule of thumb and is especially for larger more conservative organizations who typically lack the skills and expertise for digital disruption, or who do not have the time to build and nurture these skills.

Complexity of transformation is divesting of an organization or part of a business that is not very transformative as it vanishes, all the way through to using real-time data to create a new business model. A highly complex transformation of an organization redefines operations with a completely new customer

journey, a completely new business model, and likely a completely new internal operating model as well. That's what we mean by complex transformation. However, such complex transformations will cause disruptions both internally and externally.
Understanding the values of internal versus external disruption is also critical to calibrating the type of transformation you have.

If the digital transformation is something innovative and creative and it has the "wow" factor, then it is going to be a huge source of energy, and it will attract a lot of energy. People will want to join that program. On the other hand, a transformation that's about cutting costs is very negative and could drain energy in the environment.

There are two types of organizations: those that are visionary and leading the way and those that are paralyzed and not quite sure what to do. The first one has a vision, anticipates consumer needs, and is probably creating the market for their consumers and those needs. The other organization is typically in a state of fear or panic, and its position is based on fear. That's a very different position than one based on a vision.

People often make changes when they don't like what they see or recognize the problems they are facing. An individual or a group of people existing in a state of fear will be very different than a person or a group of people that has a vision of where they want to go. Many companies fear disrupting their business models, which leads to insecurities that impact the quality of their decisions. Lack of facts impacts speed and output and past experiences impact confidence. The feeling of 'lack of' as opposed to abundance leads them to be unable to communicate with conviction.

Takeaways here include:
- Lesson 1: Understand Chasm Theory and the concept of 'whole product'
- Lesson 2: Short-circuit the approach to get to the customer value as quickly as possible
- Lesson 3: While the whole organization is running a long marathon (existing business), peel off the sprinters to run the 100-meter race
- Lesson 4: Know who your stakeholders are— all of them!
- Lesson 5: Have a 'move towards' strategy which is based on a positive vision of the future you want to create, not a 'move away from' one that is based on fear.

CHAPTER 2: The 5 Disruption Levers

When you look at the ineffective execution of going digital, there are some very clear inhibitors: lack of experience, lack of leadership that translates to lack of vision and strategy, lack of IT skills, inability to stay ahead of emerging business models and lack of business analyst skills. The market is moving too fast, and organizations are unable to react. For smart-services-focused digital disruption, there is also the impact to hardware engineering to consider and the lead time for manufacturing. Many organizations are confused about which partners to work with and are left wondering if they should work with Systems Integrator's or Management Consultancies and how much to do internally versus externally. Choosing the wrong partner can be a recipe for disaster. There is typically minimal consideration of customer experience, so organizations don't necessarily put the customer absolutely at the center of everything they do. This is probably one of the biggest mistakes that organizations make and why they don't meet the digital goals they set.

They also rely heavily on older IT data systems that aren't evolving for mobile or the Cloud. Many parts of your organization—technology, processes, etc.—need to change. The impact to change affects many parts of your organization, so your risks are very high. For all of this to come together—to get the orchestra to think harmoniously and play music together—is very difficult. It's that complexity that gives rise to risks; **therefore, we call going digital a digital gamble.**

The 5 Disruption Levers

Let's look back at the two types of organizations: those in a state of panic and those that are visionary. The business of organizations in a state of panic is not going to stay the same. The organization will spiral downward because competitors are moving faster and consumers' expectations are beyond what their systems and their customer experience can deliver.

The opposite of the vicious cycle is the virtuous cycle. You hit a little bit of success, which breeds a little more success, and so on. You spiral upwards and there's an incredible change in the success of the company.

How do you build a virtuous cycle that leads you to success? You structure the company conversation in five areas that we refer to as the "The 5 Disruption Levers."

These 5 disruption levers are defined and discussed more in-depth later in the book, but they are:
1. The Digital Culture

2. The Digital Leader
3. The Operating Model Strategy
4. The Customer Experience
5. Hardware, Data and the Cloud

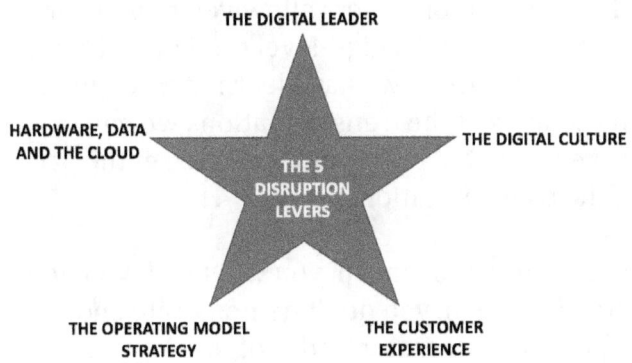

These are the five areas that need to come together to truly deliver the transformation required to bring Smart Services to market. It is the optimal balancing of these levers that will dictate the relevancy of your enterprises products and services in this fourth industrial revolution. If you structure your company's execution around these five areas, you prioritize risks and opportunities in a very clear and concise way, so people can clearly see the objective, discuss the data, and get behind them. Also, all parts of the organization understand their roles for these initiatives. For instance, the call center team that deals with customer satisfaction knows exactly what it is responsible for, and so does the R&D team, the technology team under the Business or IT or supply chain and field operations under the operating model. Everyone is driving to the same goal and knows what their goal is.

The 5 Disruption Levers allow you to build an organization and a high-level road map. This is critical. One thing we have learned throughout the courses of the transformations we have driven is that it's very important to set the pace of the transformation.

If you bite off too much, you will fail. If you don't bite off enough, you don't demonstrate enough value. Therefore, as a leader of the transformation, calibrating and pacing the organization in these five areas is absolutely critical for reaching the success you want. As with anything, you have to deliver results quickly, but you are better off biting off small chunks, showing success, and moving on to the next chunk, climbing in a virtuous cycle. That's what we're trying to do.

The 5 Disruption Levers allow you to consider how digitally mature your organization is, which then tells you how to pace its change. If it is very immature, change is going to take longer.

The main thing you need to understand about the 5 Disruption Levers is that any one of the levers can be exercised first as your entry into disruption. For instance, your organization could gravitate first to ideas around potential business model changes that can increase net new revenue, which could lead to continuous innovation on an existing product or service or creating a brand-new product or service. It could be that you have enough feedback from customers that your organization decides to embark on a continuous innovation roadmap, which has the potential to impact your business and operating models.

As the key enabler of the digital transformation, it is your responsibility to:
1. Bring together the five disruption levers, so the right people across the organization are speaking to each other, are aware of each other's work, and are leveraging each other's work to inform their own disruption component
2. Help shape and align the priorities of each component. For the program to be successful, a clear roadmap needs to be defined for each of the components. A clear digital business roadmap should have a crawl, walk, and run strategy, along with scope for each prioritized item.
3. Create and publish a joint timeline, bringing together the five aspects that anyone can see across the organization
4. Communicate the plan through effective governance and program management

5. Select the right set of partners to assist you through the journey

CHAPTER 3: The Digital Culture

Diagnosis for Digital Maturity

Organizations are just like people in how they learn, change, and adapt. A well-known learning matrix is shown below. It's a great idea to use this to assess the maturity of your organization. We have adapted it a bit to make it more relevant. It is imperative to know the state of your organization, so you can adopt the appropriate approach and provide the right leadership at the right time. We use the following framework to be clear on where the starting point is.

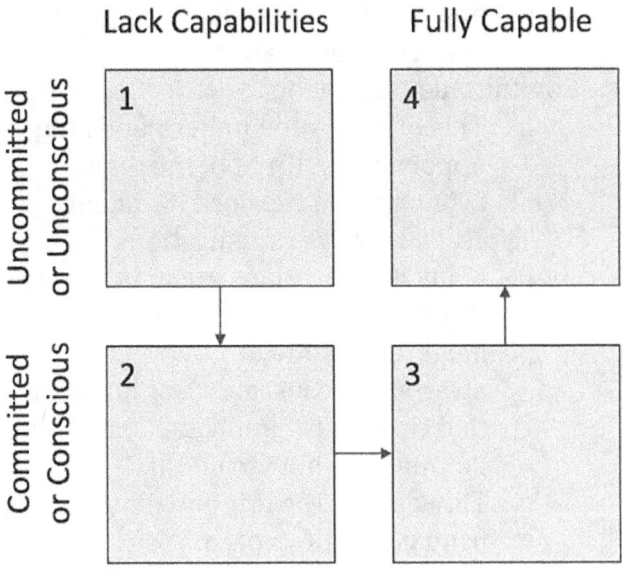

1. Uncommitted or Unconscious + Lacks Capabilities
   a. These organizations are asleep at the wheel. Look for signs of an aging product line that hasn't changed much. If this product is a cash cow and continues to be, the organization can become lazy or just comfortable.
   b. Low staff churn
   c. Markets with high barriers to entry
   d. Signs will be messaging around: "We are shielded from this digital impacts because…"
   e. Traditional product development process with long range roadmaps and top down decision making on feature prioritization
2. Committed or Conscious + Lacks Capabilities
   a. This organization understands the opportunity/threat of the digital economy and the need for change Typically reactive organizations
   b. Many organizations are in this state
   c. Quite a few organizations live in this heightened state of awareness/consciousness knowing that they 'must' innovate to stay alive, but not sure how to do this.
   d. Think about the top-down messaging from your CEO/board. What adjectives describe the mood; paralysed, fearful, reactive, do-or-die?

3. Committed or Conscious + Developing Capabilities
   a. This organization understands the opportunity/threat of the digital economy and the need for change
   b. It typically anticipates the digital disruption and is on a journey of building its digital capabilities
   c. It's worth exploring the level of capabilities the company truly has because many organizations fall into the trap of believing they are capable but are not. Therefore, their digital programs don't meet intended outcomes.
   d. Implemented or implementing 'Agile Safe 4.0' as well as design thinking for experimentation led product development
4. Uncommitted or Unconscious + Full Capabilities
   a. There are very few organizations in this space, given the digital disruption has just begun
   b. Healthy paranoia technology or business model disruption

Once you have diagnosed where your organization is, how committed it is, and its level of capability or digital maturity, what do you do next?

CHAPTER 4: The Digital Leader

If we consider where organizations are in their digital evolution as the starting point, digital transformation of this digital economy has just begun. There is a long journey ahead of all of us. The digital economy is going to change the way you do business.

Let's say you are in an organization that is uncommitted or unconscious, probably lacking capability in IT. If you were fully committed and fully capable, there would be several things you could visualize. You could probably visualize a chief digital officer, an innovation team, innovation labs, and innovation processes, and you would see them experimenting unashamedly.

Unfortunately, this isn't the case for most organizations. Very few organizations have all this DNA already established; the majority are trying to build, acquire, or create this DNA. How do you build leadership? In some cases, this is driven from the top down; the CEO will recognize the importance of the digital economy. But most CEOs are worried about the stock market, total shareholder value, today's revenue, and new bookings. A lot of their focus is on making the number today, and may not be afforded the luxury of looking outside of that. Although there's a high level of awareness, but how many CEOs are investing in these new digital areas sufficiently with their dollars and management attention?

We've found that there are typically entrepreneurs within the company who are free-thinkers, mavericks, and visionaries. They have done a lot of reading and have passion and energy around the digital economy. You may be one of these people; after all, you're reading this book! Maybe you're part of an organization where there's nobody at a senior level who has gotten organized around how to address the digital economy and the opportunities and risks it presents.

If you are a free-thinker, how do you start influencing? First, congratulate yourself, and recognize that you have an opportunity to become a leader. You have to assume authority. Part of doing this lies in your own self-belief and self-confidence. If you don't believe fully in the opportunities you see, you're going to struggle to assume authority.

What do we mean by "authority?" Authority means you can have conversations with key stakeholders about the business. Nothing stops you from picking up the phone, talking to the secretary of a senior manager in the business, and getting them to talk to you; inviting somebody senior to one of your presentations;

or attending one of their team meetings from a learning perspective. There are many ways to become an authority in the digital economy and the opportunity the digital world offers.

First, you should both formally and informally present yourself as the visionary who sees where the organization could go. There's no doubt that people—including people in leadership positions—will start to recognize you as such. Word-of-mouth is probably the best way for you to gain authority in this particular area. We're referring to organizations that don't have a top-down approach, wherein the CEO appoints somebody to take the lead. We get it, even in most cases somebody who is a COO, running a highly non-digital business is chartered to go and drive a digital smart service initiative but do they have the passion, the energy, the vision to go and do it successfully?

How do you become empowered? The only way to gain empowerment is to ask somebody who has access to budget resources or can allow for management attention. Eventually, there will come an inflection point when you will have to spend more formal time building the case for going digital, but, in most cases, this will be a step-by-step approach. It's important for your immediate manager to be aware of what you're doing. Without their support, you have to be careful about being a maverick because if your boss feels threatened, you're going to have issues. Support from your immediate manager gives you a level of cover; you can start gaining empowerment to speak out more, share your thought leadership, and create further thought leadership.

Creating a Case for Action

Once you do become a self-proclaimed evangelist or leader, you need to create the case for action. To do this, need to have something relevant to say. Based on the 5 Disruption Levers, we know that getting success in digital transformation is a huge gamble; the stakes are high, and the risks are high. Executives understand the risk associated with any investment in going digital. If you are positioning yourself as a leader, you can't speak generally about the digital economy and being disrupted. You need to speak credibly and with depth about two to three of the Disruption Levers by presenting opportunities. You are more likely to gain momentum if you bring forward fact-based insights about opportunities, rather than fear.

People with fear have the potential to be paralyzed, but if your ideas present opportunity, and there's a dollar figure associated with them, like net new revenue and organic growth, then those ideas will win in the end. Risk of going out of business, risk of losing customers, or just cutting costs and saving money are not how you lead the conversation. Articulating all of the Disruption Levers clearly is critical.

Once you have the thought leadership, the credibility, and something relevant to say, the next step is to start building relationships, which will come in all shapes and sizes. We have seen examples of successful alliances between a thought-leader and a developer halfway across the globe, or someone in a call-center team who's dealing with customer complaints, or someone who deals with customer insight and surveys. Going to some of these teams and individuals who are subject-matter experts at the operational level and starting to build alliances with them will further enhance the credibility of your skills. The more fact-based and grounded your arguments are, the better you will be at pitching your idea.

It's important to increase your awareness of your organization's operating model. These are the methods, processes, and tools through which your company delivers the promise of your product or service to its customers. The ability for you to link the operating model with profit and loss (P&L) is significant because it creates credibility, especially with the CFO and senior executives. Once you start to build these relationships, you start to build a coalition of people who are credible in their own fields and can get behind your idea.

If you are a middle-manager or a senior manager, you could directly request resources for your initiative or get them indirectly assigned to your initiative. This depends on the culture and DNA of your organization and is something we've done successfully. It starts to create a virtual team with a nucleus. The nucleus is a center of excellence for digital thinking. When multiple disciplines feed into that nucleus, you will start to see your credibility and the credibility of the virtual team shoot through the roof.

One final point on this is about politics. The stakes are very high when it comes to digital transformation. People's careers are potentially on the line, profits are on the line, the brand of the company is on the line, etc. A great technical idea or a great customer journey will be disruptive to internal dynamics. The sooner you can find and enlist a mentor to support you and give you the political air cover, the better you will fair. Find a mentor who understands the culture and the politics of the organization.

CHAPTER 5: The Customer Experience

Digital disruption with Smart services starts with the customer at the center. How do you determine effectively and objectively what your consumers and your customers want? What will entertain them, excite them, and inspire them? Before starting the ideation and designing the customer journey, it is important to put the human experience at the beginning. Interrogating customers and empathizing with them is what should jumpstart the imaginative process.

Voice of the Customer

Many organizations have formal programs around receiving voice of the customer or the voice of the partner. These are great ways to collect feedback about how your customers want to interact with you, how they want to engage with you, and what needs they have that you can fulfill. If you do not have such a program in place today, our suggestion is to get that program underway by creating customer success teams or extending that function within your call center teams or through other methods like customer facing surveys or sales or pre-sales teams. You need to get information from your customers, so they can validate your ideas or provide further insight into those ideas.

Strategy Team
Another way to get the voice of the customer and understand the desired customer experience is to understand where you are today and how you compare to global standards and your competitors, while defining upfront requirements and defining initial strategic recommendations. Most organizations have some function within their product or service organization that is responsible for defining future strategy. These teams are also well-equipped with industry data and business analytics that analyze past performance while predicting potential future outcomes, including potential new investments that the organization should consider or processes that can be improved. Knowing who the strategy team is and engaging them helps shape the customer experience as well.

Validating Concepts
Another way to understand and put customers in the center is to perform end-user research. Taking ideas and vetting them in real scenarios is an important strategy for forming what your initial priorities for your product or service need to be. That's exactly where experimentation, creation of early concepts, and validation of those concepts come into play. In order to create early concepts, it is important to have initial funding available and some level of consensus built between you, product management, and

operations to ensure you can go from a validated concept to a full program without a lot of friction. Validating experiments needs to be part of your New Product Introduction (NPI) strategy.

Defining the Customer Experience Map
Whatever your vision for your smart service is, as you get it validated by various audiences, you want to build the Customer Experience Map. According to the *Harvard Business Review*, a customer journey map is a very simple idea. It's a diagram that illustrates the steps your customer(s) go through in engaging with your company, whether it be through a product, an online experience, a retail experience, a service, or any combination of those. The more touchpoints you have, the more complicated— but necessary—a Customer Experience Map becomes.

The Minimum Viable Experience (MVE)
The first set of prioritized experiences defines the Minimum Viable Experience (MVE) that you expect to deliver as part of the launch of your smart service. Be clear though, how you define 'viable'. We have seen that teams sometimes base this on the enterprise's needs as opposed to what the customer will 'love'. Launching prematurely without enough to get the customer to love your smart service could be an expensive endeavor.

The Smart Service Business Roadmap

Once you've identified a series of priorities along with your MVE, you will start defining the maturity model from a customer perspective. This is how you envision your customers to interact and engage with you. It is key to tie the various steps in your Customer Experience Map to your operating model. For every step in the Customer Experience Map, you should map what the impact to the operating model will be. This includes any new processes or modifications to existing processes or tools that will be required to handle the desired customer experience.

The third dimension to the business roadmap is your business model, which dictates how you plan to meet your financial outcomes. Eventually, the Smart Service Business Roadmap will show the prioritized Customer Experience Map over time tied to operating model and business model impacts.

The outcome from this exercise of putting the customer in the center is your Smart Service Business Roadmap, which is something you should be able to share with your executives, with your strategic partners, and with various other operational teams, and even get feedback directly from your customers themselves.

CHAPTER 6: The Operating Model Strategy

Everybody's 'Mental Map of the World' is Different

Transformation, innovation and disruption are such grand words. A title with any of those in it is very enviable. Once your idea is in motion, your organization's board is excited, the executive sponsor is excited, and the team is excited. Some of the stakeholders, however, may not be so thrilled.

Do you know who the stakeholders are, why they may not be thrilled, and what influence they have directly and/or indirectly on your initiative? An important question to ask is how your end-users or customers feel about your transformation. These stakeholders are what we call, your 'success-holders,' as they all stand to benefit from the success of the initiative.

This approach ensures that you think through what success looks like to each of these communities or individuals. If you can't articulate clearly how the success threads through your organization and the financials of your customers, you have a problem; you are leaving a weak link in the chain for someone to pull on. The more work done upfront to get deep with each of the success-holders and understand what success looks like to them specifically will pay dividends many times over. Document what they say, even using their exact words, and read or play it back to them. This is your chance to create an emotional contract.

Transformation or 'Trans-Continuum'
The grand plan is drawn up, and the large, multi-functional team is assembled. Where do you begin, and when do you see success? We have seen huge expectations laid at the doorsteps of teams that very quickly realize that the huge magnitude of what is required will take time, but the sponsors are impatient and want to see the benefits as quickly as possible.

Transformation inherently means something new; it requires innovation. There has been much research into innovation, and one of the key findings is that most people 'feel their way' through to the most potent idea or ideas. The path is not linear, but a meandering one of U-turns. It sometimes fades away completely. Therefore, it is important to agree upfront with sponsors and success-holders on what the journey will be like and some of the stop-off points for reflection or rest, during this journey of experimentation.

Innovating is all about playing with our tools: hands, hearts, and minds. Do you recall playing with toys when you were a child and inventing characters and stories? Innovating is like that.

Creativity is fun! The question is whether your environment is ready, willing, and able to allow it to happen. There must be a safe environment for the inventor or the people who are experimenting to be free of expectation, so their creative juices can flow.

For larger, more structured corporate initiatives, it is critical to set the pace of the transformation correctly. Far too often, sponsors have unrealistic expectations because no one is brave enough to set the record straight in terms of how complex it is to drive wide-scale transformation. It is better to break down the transformation into a series of mini-projects with quicker evidence of success. However, in today's fast-paced economy, it takes wisdom and confidence to size and pace a transformation, particularly when there are financial pressures.

| 'SUCCESS BELIEFS' | 'SUCCESS-HOLDERS' | | | | |
	Customers	End Users	Executive Sponsor	Board	Financial Controller
Effort Required increases or decreases?					
Financial Gain or Loss?		✓			
Reputation enhancer or destroyer?					
Pacing - too fast or too slow?					
My future position - Strengthened or weakened?					
How important is the outcome to me?					

Well-Formed Customer Engagement Outcomes

A key component of transformation is the definition of well-formed outcomes. Success holders have varying beliefs about what success is. The CFO may see it as financial, while the Sales VP or the Services VP may be see it as building customer loyalty or putting in place a loss leader to attract further revenue down the line. In terms of outcome, and depending on the map of the world we pulled our digital transformation from, success is very different from person to person.

Think about well-formed outcomes by describing with your senses what the outcomes will be. The questions would be: What does the success look like? What will you see with your eyes? What will people see? What will you hear? What will you hear people talking about, whether it's the press, an analyst, in a meeting, etc.? You have to also consider what people would feel—what emotions would come up—when describing what's new about this.

Think about the additional benefits or gains from the outcome. Training the outcome so it's well formed is critical to success because if not everyone agrees on what that success is, it's never going to be successful.

Business Model: Mapping Customer Experience with Potential Monetization Opportunities

The first alignment that needs to happen is between the customer experience and the potential monetization opportunities. Potential monetization opportunities have to be clearly defined and articulated, along with specific numbers that can be assigned, assumed, or formally defined for various teams within the organization.

From the customer standpoint, the maturity model should have an overlay that defines what the appropriate business model innovation will be over that period of time. In the first set of product innovation with a certain set of capabilities, you may choose to introduce a subscription-based payment offering, evolving that into an add-on set of services like pay-per-use or pay-per-outcome, or like proactive warranty offerings based on the next set of capabilities that you unlock in your product or service or even white label scenarios. You may also have options on the go-to-market strategy for the product based on its roadmap, perhaps through a channel for a certain period or bypassing the channel in some cases. Then, as more customers from certain geographical areas or categories come onboard, you evolve that into a more direct relationship.

Those types of decisions have to be made at that moment in time and have to be aligned with how the customers will evolve in the future. Socialization and alignment with each part of the business is critical. Monetization or the route to market from the sales perspective needs to be considered because there's only a limited amount of sales capacity that an organization has, be it number of salespeople, number of partner channel managers, or even payable commissions. If you're going to feed your new innovative product or service through that channel, are they going to accept it and have the capacity to deal with it? How easy will it be for them to sell and make money from it? All these considerations are key, and alignment needs to happen early and clearly for success to be realized.

Business Operations and Internal Productivity

The next aspect of operating-model optimization is on business operations and your internal productivity. You have your customer journey, you have the business model and its evolution that ties to the customer journey. At the heart of all this, there's going to be an impact on how your organization works to enable those things to come alive. Fundamentally, you need to consider things like how customers are on-boarded to this new product or service and how you manage intake of orders. Traditionally, people had to fill out a form and take many other steps to get an order in. Now, the backend processes may enable a customer to directly enjoy the product or service. Is there a change in the way you provide or support warranties? How will field-service personnel react to work orders? How will revenue be accounted for and accrued over time? These are all real challenges that require and concise action plans.

One way to identify which operations will be impacted by this transformation journey is to map them to the customer journey itself. Not only are you mapping the customer journey and the business model, you're also showing what operations need to be modified, changed, or enhanced and when this will happen. You have to be able to articulate to your success holder the organization's plan to support this new transformation. For example, it might be that certain elements of the operation will have a crawl strategy because some of the underlying IT systems are not able to handle a change in a certain type of a process. For other operations, you may have a walk strategy, meaning you can digitize some parts of a process as we are able to execute that operation relatively painlessly, from a systems perspective, processes perspective, and enablement perspective.

This alignment of the mapping of the customer journey to the operating process inside the company teases out the critical dependency. As you work on this mapping exercise, you'll find those critical dependencies and the areas that need to be addressed.

Because you are looking at the journey and the innovative product you want to take to market, you'll also get a sense of timing. Things can't happen overnight, and each of these functions has their own set of priorities. How do you ensure that everyone is on the same page? If you decided that your Minimum Viable Experience (MVE) was "X", but now it's "X" minus "N" because certain aspects of the experience can't come alive in the timelines for the MVE, will your success holders still define the MVE as a success? You might find that certain parts of the organization are able to deliver something that you need to adjust for the MVE, or maybe part of the organization can deliver more than you expected. Without having this structure, it's very difficult to create a sense of prioritization and teamwork to get the product or service to market.

Data Gaps

The third major consideration for operating-model optimization is data. Every organization has its own maturity around what data it has, how it gets the data, how trustworthy the data is, how it can use that data, and how it can feed intelligence from an insight based on that data to various people in the organization.

Almost every organization has data gaps. The goal of the transformation program is to clearly identify data elements that prevent the transformation from successfully taking place. It's the ability to define upfront what data would be needed that isn't currently available.

One key area of data gap is a concept called Installed Base. The Installed Base allows an organization to tie all data related to a particular product or service and look at it from the entire lifestyle of that product or service—from the moment it was manufactured, to when it was assembled, to when it was sold, to when it was delivered and installed at a customer site and when it was serviced. This includes constantly capturing information like the parts that were added to it, hardware and software features that were added at a later time, upgrades, and repairs. You'll know exactly what product and what SKU it was, exactly which customer it was, exactly which distributor sold it was, and exactly the serial numbers and work orders associated with it. Having that 360-degree view around the lifecycle of the product and its journey— including its touchpoints with customers, partners, backend systems, and field engagement—is critical. Therefore, making sure that the organization has confidence in its master data about its products, customers, and suppliers is an important part of the data strategy.

Depending on the size of your organization, you'll need to use the concept of bundles, wherein different components are bundled together in a specific SKU. When order entry was first implemented, it may have been implemented with a particular bundle offered at that time. Unfortunately, offers, SKUs, and bundles are continually evolving. The dimensions keep changing because new offers are introduced. Typically, you can review the master data over time and compare and contrast it, but this also adds more complexity.

One element of the operating model that you have to be able to capture is the cost of making those changes, just as the business model captures the potential revenue, the number of new customers, and the amount of net new revenue. Similarly, from an operating perspective, you have to be clear on exactly what it's going to cost to make changes. That's the level of clarity you need for the program to be successfully funded and successfully engage people.

The Investment Model
As you prepare the business case for your smart services, it is imperative that you provide a 360-degree view of investment to senior executives. Missing key aspects of investment will erode their confidence in you and the transformation program. You will also need to consider how

your organization plans to fund the investment for year one and the following years. Key concepts you should familiarize yourself with include whether cost should be expensed or capitalized initially? How should year 2 costs be considered? Including financial analysts through the journey will allow you to create a stronger financial plan that will pass the scrutiny of the CFO. Eventually getting deep into the Profit and Loss (P&L) and the operating model will be a key differentiator as people say "Show me the money". You'll be able to answer the CFO's question one minute and the operations teams' question the next minute – this will gain you immediate credibility. One key consideration of making the business case work and demonstrate Return on Investment (ROI) is to consider leveraging Infrastructure as a Service (IaaS), Platform as a Service (PaaS), Software as a Service (SaaS) for lower capital investments upfront. In fact, XaaS (Anything as a Service) should be the first consideration as far as investment is concerned. Therefore, it is important that you spend the time to understand the levers available for how the investment will be accounted for by the organization

There are four key areas of investment that you should be prepared to include and present as part of your business case. They are shown below:

The Investment Plan

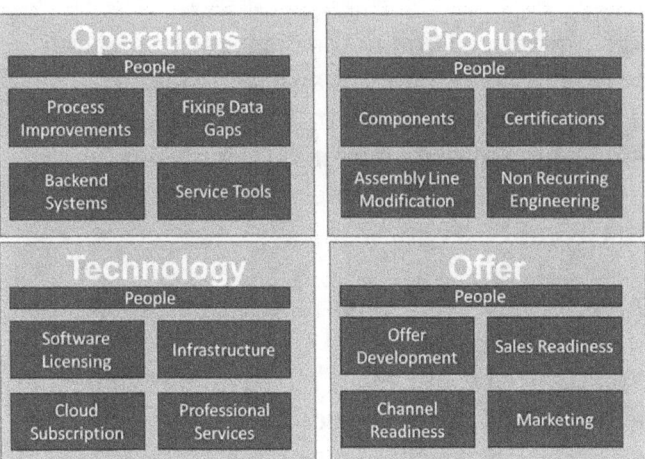

Building Digital Momentum – People, People, People

There are three things that matter when considering any major transformation: people, people, people. With the advent of cloud providers offering fast set-up times and subscription pricing, the technical and process risk has been considerably reduced, and flexibility has increased. It comes down to the group's collective expectations of the transformation, as well as their willingness to offer their creative energy. Without the success holders acting as a true team, the business change is doomed from the outset. We can site numerous examples of how people consciously or subconsciously sabotage an initiative by not being sincere about their contributions.

We introduced you to the term success holder earlier. A stakeholder is a success holder.
The language is important as having a stake in something infers a part investments versus holding the success, which infers being linked to the overall success.

Another new term is for metrics: Success metrics = success beliefs.
You want to think about the customer value and about which problems boil to the surface as the critical most potent ideas or use cases and exploit them within your experiment keeping the customer experience values in mind. You start with what some would called "minimum viable product" and others call "minimum payable product," what is going to get traction and create value with your customer. That's what we try to do when we think about the considerations we make for our experiments.

Many of you will have your own set of metrics, which should be as quantitative as possible. This is very helpful for mathematical outcomes, such a financial metrics. The danger is that whether something is deemed a success or not can be determined by what people 'believe' about the initiative, as well as what it has achieved.

Something that is commonly used in NLP is the process of creating a well-formed outcome. This involves going beyond the dry metrics and establishing the relationship people will have with outcome; how they will feel about it. This is important because, as humans, we are emotional beings. We want to feel good about an outcome. What makes people feel good varies quite a bit.

We have a model we use to create an emotional heat map that uses both of these concepts: stakeholders = success-holders and success metrics = success beliefs. Connect with us to learn more about this.

IT or Not IT?
As your organization experiences the learning curve of how to seize digital opportunities or how to deal with the threat of new entrants or competitors, your CIO be heavily focused on re-inventing his or her team to stay relevant to the key business issues. This is not easy, as the existing team may not be able to change or grow as quickly enough to meet the urgent business demands.

In addition, all the new-age Cloud, IoT, and digital agencies and consultancies are doing their utmost to get to the business leaders who drive the change or deal with the digital transformation. There is a risk that the IT team becomes alienated due to a lack of value contribution.

Furthermore, many organizations have appointed chief digital officers (CDO). The enterprises who are serious will see the CDO as a peer to the CIO and CSO. A true CDO will be a customer champion more than a technology champion (CIO) or a total shareholder return (TSR) champion (CSO).

On the flip side, CIO ambitions are at an all-time high as the business is moving in their direction, increasing their power. This clearly is a threat to the business leader who may feel alienated and personally at risk of losing power or even worse his/her job.

How do you deal with this crowded space? Look at the complexity of the transformation. If you are operating at the higher level of our transformation hierarchy, then you would either hire a true CDO and empower this individual or move the CIO into this position if he/she has the personal ambition to fulfil the role. If you are operating at the lower levels of the hierarchy, then it is critical to take the CIO and IT team with you on the journey. Every case is unique and will also depend upon the organizational culture.

How to build collaboration warrants a whole book unto itself!

How to Get People to Love Your Idea

When you consider going digital, the best practice is to go through a course of experimentation, which de-risks the gamble. If you have a big bang, the stakes are high, you're taking a big risk. How do you reduce the level of the gamble you are taking? You take more steps, and you experiment by trial and error. As long as you have support, you've created an environment for your digital ideas, you've enlisted a mentor, and you have your coalition built to get after the transformation, then you'll want to experiment.

- People don't always make decisions in a logical way. They make decisions using their hearts, minds, and guts, with a varying degree of emphasis. Loyalty is created when people make decisions from the heart and the gut and less from the mind. These emotional decisions are stronger and will be the topics of referral conversations.
- Maintaining and building rapport with your potential or existing customers is paramount. There are extensive statistics that demonstrate that friendly customer service and how people feel and are treated when interacting with an organization has a huge impact on customer loyalty and indeed

whether they choose to become a customer in the first place. It just takes one breakage in rapport to create a detractor rather than a loyal customer.

- Say what you do, and do what you say. Whatever expectations you set for your customer experience, meet them fully. There is no point setting unrealistic expectations and risking not meeting them.

- In this day of visual overload, it is imperative that companies' websites, branding, and advertising are eye-catching and creative, allowing the organization to stand out from the crowd.

- Active content on social media, including blogging and posting on Twitter and Facebook creates a positive feeling toward the organization and can build trust.

- Have a visible and active customer complaints and feedback process that is easily accessible through all channels to market. An example is British Telecom's "high-level complaints process," which is run out of the chairman's office.

This chapter discussed four key things that need to happen:

1. Provide clarity about and align the business model to the customer journey.
2. Align the operating model and impacting operations. For each impacted operation,

have a strategy for how it will be addressed while aligning it to the customer journey.

3. Understand the data gaps and the system gaps, and align those to the customer journey.

4. Create a compelling investment model.

These areas are critical to ensuring progress; road mapping these things will give you confidence in your plan and will be required for executives to sign off on such a transformation journey. Without this level of clarity, it will not be possible.

CHAPTER 7: Hardware, Data and the Cloud

Product innovation is the fifth of the Disruption Levers. At this point, you have made significant progress on your customer journey, your business model, and your operating model. Now you have to think about how that translates to impacting your product strategy.

There are two major shifts influencing product innovation. Each builds the other's case for inclusion as part of your product innovation strategy. One is a connected product, and the second is the adoption of Cloud platform services. You need to consider how these come together for product innovation that drives Smart Services.

Connected Product Innovation

Product and service innovation can come in many different flavors. There are products that need changes to their hardware and industrial design, and there are services that rely on real-time information from a connected product. There might be software that you write that enhances your current products to better diagnose and predict issues. All of these are sources of transformation specific to how your customers will interact and engage with you in the future.

You may be a hardware company and know your hardware very well, but the emerging electrical engineering options and Cloud technology might not be well known to you. You may be a software, Cloud, or application company that wants to launch hardware products. The key point we are trying to make here is that there are at least two different worlds colliding now.

As far as connected products or services is concerned, we will assume that you are a hardware product company, looking for product and service innovation to unleash digital opportunities based on your potential customer experience and monetization opportunities. You will need to ensure that from a product-engineering perspective, your set of actions are completely aligned with your customer experience and operating model roadmap and journey.

If you want to go digital and connect your hardware to the Internet, you suddenly have four parallel streams of activity that need to come together.

Turning a Stand-Alone Product Into a Connected Product – The Device

For industrial hardware manufacturing companies that cater to B2B or B2C markets, there are significant implications to hardware engineering depending on their maturity and understanding of advances in electrical engineering, their in-house design and development capabilities, their experience with Cloud platforms, and their software development expertise. Before you can turn your stand-alone product into a Cloud-connected product, you must evaluate the impact to the mechanical and electrical engineering of your product, software development, certification, manufacturing, and assembly, as shown in the image below.

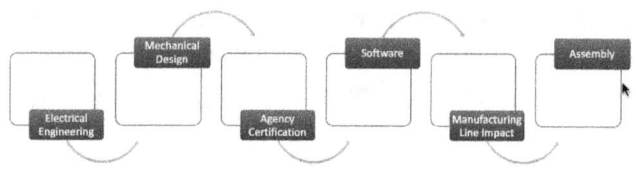

There are two ways to approach the evolution of your hardware product to a connected product:

1. **Custom Design Services Method**
   One option for redesigning your product for digital opportunities is to consult a design company that provides engineering services and assists with mechanical reengineering; electrical design; certification; and custom controller board design using custom, off-the-shelf (COTS) components. These companies do not offer products, which means they do not have manufacturing capacity; however, they do have partnerships

they can work within to get product sub-assembly.

2. **Third-Party Product Integration Method**
   A newer opportunity is to work with a product company that makes embeddable, Cloud-connected microprocessors or controllers that can be incorporated in your product. There has been a significant rise in the innovation in this area. Most companies in this space offer mechanical and electrical design services while also creating custom controller boards to fit your hardware product. These companies focus on design to manufacturing and design to assembly, and provide manufacturing, certification, warranty, and support. Their goal is not to generate revenue from services rather from embedding their products in yours.

Which option is good for you depends on your time to market, your product requirements, your customer experience, your cost, and your organization's ability to adapt.

Overall, you need to think about your time to market, as that will be important to compare to your roadmap for the customer journey, the business model, and the operating model, since it has implications for the entire program and its timeline.

Smart Services Application Development
A connected product is one that is either a brand-new product that you envision communicating to the Cloud and therefore allowing and enabling Smart services innovation, or a traditionally stand-alone product that is transformed into a connected product as well.

Now we'll discuss the various components that make up the anatomy of a connected product and the applications that deliver the digital experience for the smart services.

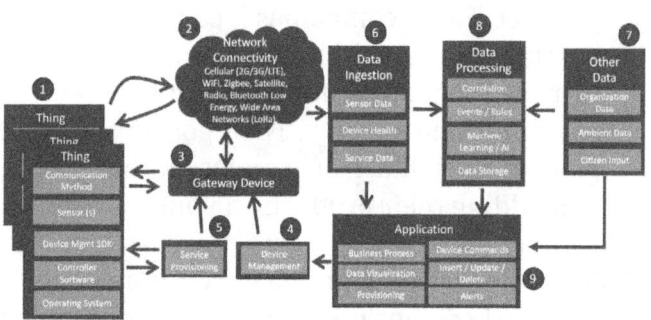

1. The Thing
    - The first component of the connected solution is the device itself. The device is your current product or the brand-new product that you're building. Within the product, there is capability for the product to communicate to the Cloud. The specific areas that enable that within a particular product first need to include some communication method that the

product will use to communicate with the Cloud.

- The product may have one or more sensors. For instance, industrial products may have sensors that record the number of revolutions of a bearing, sense the temperature in soil, or measure the strength of one machine hitting another as part of a manufacturing process. These are all sensors that capture data. There might be one or more sensors in your product.
- The third component inside the product is the device management software development kit. The device management software development kit enables the product to register with the cloud IoT platform, authenticate and establish bidirectional communications securely.
- The controller software is the fourth component on the product. It allows the sensors and other functions on the device itself to collect data from the sensors and perform functions on the device.
- Finally, there is an operating system on the device itself. This could be a selection of the real-time operating systems (RTOS) or fundamental, single-board computers that come with the real-time operating system.

2. The second component of the connected product is the network itself. There is a

significant amount of innovation that is occurring currently on the methods for enabling a device to connect and more importantly communicate over a standard protocol that aids in building truly Smart Services.

3. In cases where the device cannot connect directly to the Cloud, there are opportunities to introduce a gateway device that acts as a medium between the device and the network. A gateway device would give you some level of ability to communicate with the Cloud. Whether it's a device that's connecting to the Cloud or the gateway device that's connecting to the Cloud, there are some fundamental functions that need to be performed.

4. One of the key elements is the idea of device management—knowing that the devices are out in the field, whether they are running, what software version they're running, what firmware upgrades are required, and which devices have already gone through firmware upgrades.

5. Another element is service provisioning. If the device specifically uses cellular connectivity, then there has to be some mechanism to provision what kind of service level that device has, its ability to perform the SMS function, and what kind of data plan it has. Just like on your cellphone, all of those are provisioned by your carrier based on the plan you've selected. Typically, service

provisioning has to occur for a product that uses cellular connectivity.

6. At this point, your device has been configured, and it can be managed. Service has been provisioned, and it's connecting to the cloud. That's when the magic begins. The first element is being able to ingest data. There are three types of data. The first and most important type is sensor data—the data that's captured from the sensors that are recording in real-time the types of information you are interested in measuring, and therefore enriching the customer experience. Again, this could be one or more sensors. One single device could have multiple sensors on it, and you could receive multiple streams of information from each sensor at any interval of time you feel is important to delivering value to your end consumers.

   The second type of data that gets ingested is the device health, which could be a simple heartbeat letting you know that the device is up and running.

   The third type of data is service data that lets you know exactly how much of the data plan, for instance, has been utilized.

7. Data coming from the connected product does not necessarily identify the customer, the location, the product hierarchy, etc. This is where correlating this enterprise metadata with real-time data coming from sensors can

provide further context and insight into a specific customer scenario. Also, combining ambient data sources available via Cloud subscriptions and data markets can add further context to the sensor data.

8. Once the data is ingested, the next logical thing to do with it is process it. A significant level of innovation in the Cloud space has allowed multiple streams of data to be correlated to exactly one device, connecting them to historical data while the data is in motion to understand factors that may influence customer experience or notifications that you may want to provide to your consumers that can be done in real-time.

   The rules to analyze and process this data in real-time and fork results to multiple systems or processes are critically important. Rules can be hard-coded rules or intelligent. Intelligent rules get into ideas of machine learning and artificial intelligence, wherein software automatically detects patterns of problems or opportunities and reflects them back in the relevant experiences you want your consumers to experience. At some point, the data has to be stored, and that's where a significant level of innovation has happened in the Cloud itself.

9. One final aspect of your connected product is the application itself. The application covers all of this capability and is the face of your

Smart service. Fundamentally, the application allows role-based access with the ability for your customers to assign users and roles for certain experiences with the application. The application is also how you visualize data to your consumers, how you're enabling them to be notified and alerted of the key information you believe will add convenience to their daily lives or their business processes. What kinds of commands can they issue back to the device? What other aspects of the business process can be automated within the application? Do your customers have the ability to provision the device themselves or initiate business processes directly from the application based on the data and what the data is telling you? These questions make up the cornerstone of your digital transformation coming alive.

Technology – Innovation Using Cloud Services

There are multiple cloud platforms that have evolved today and are evolving and innovating at a faster and faster pace. What we are not going to cover is one specific cloud platform. Instead, we want to highlight specific platform services that should be part of your toolbox.

Platform services or platform as a service (PaaS) is an aspect that Cloud vendors offer that allows you to develop, run, and manage applications without the need to build and maintain the infrastructure required to run your application. These are different than infrastructure as a service (IaaS) and software as a service (SaaS).

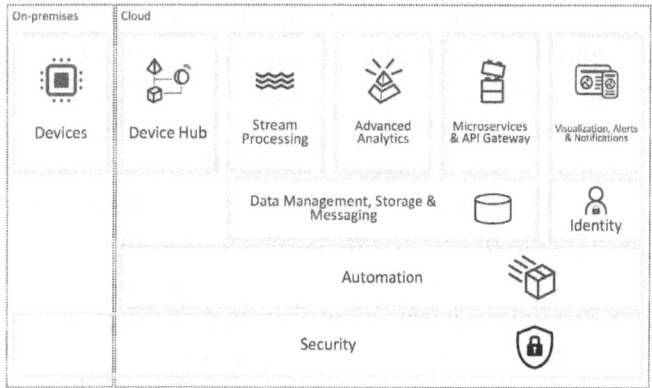

Image Courtesy – Bob Familiar, Blue Metal

Services that you should think about leveraging and using as part of your new product or service and bringing to market are discussed in the image above.

One of the key services in any Cloud platform is automation. Specifically, how can you manage these services using script, and how can you scale them up or scale them down based on rules, automating that process easily?

Securely managing the identities of consumers, partners, and B2B customers and mapping them back to your application and relevant data is critical for delivering personalized experiences.

Understanding who users are, what roles they play, and what access levels they have, and what capabilities the application enables them to perform will determine the convenience and self-service factors of your solution.

Data management storage and messaging are series of services that you should evaluate. In the data management space, specifically, there are many options related to how you want to store data. That is truly dictated by the type of data you're storing and, more importantly, what you want to do with that data. The Cloud can handle structured and unstructured data and a highly scalable relational data warehouse. Messaging services are critical for scaling how data is ingested, how data is managed, and, more importantly, how you route data to different systems and applications, so things can be performed in a connected manner.

Further, stream processing services are critically important. As more experiences depend on interpreting insights and actions from real-time information, it is important to ensure that there is some service in your Cloud platform that allows you to collect streaming data, apply rules to the streaming data, correlate that data with historical information, and either apply hard-coded rules or intelligent rules like machine learning and artificial intelligence.

The next type of service that you should actively evaluate within your Cloud platform is advanced analytics. Advanced analytics include things like machine learning; artificial intelligence; and other types of cognitive services like natural language, understanding models, facial recognition, recommendations, speech-to-text, text-to-speech, text analytics, translation, and determining emotion. All of these are services allow you to further improve, personalize, engage, predict, and proactively prevent based on real-time incoming information. You also need to consider ideas around micro-services and begin to create robust APIs that, in the future, could be monetized within your product and finally the ability for potential platform users to create fantastic visualizations, alerts, notifications and host applications.

As far as the connected product is concerned, one element of service that you should evaluate within your Cloud platform is the capability to have device registration; device connectivity; secure device provisioning; device management; management of device identity in the Cloud; and the ability to perform, command, and control bi-directional transactions. These are services that you want to ensure are available in your Cloud platform.

Security
Security is an essential enabler for any connected solution in delivering the right

experience without compromising your brand and product. Security is at the heart of the entire stack from hardware, device, cloud, data, users and your application. Below, we provide a high-level view into areas that you should consider having experts work with you for covering your entire connected solution. This list is by no means exhaustive, rather to bring awareness to you that security is comprehensive and needs to be dealt with as a specific work stream.

Your Connected Solution

Application

Secure Authorization	Identity Management
Authentication	Roles

Cloud Platform

Secure Over The Air Updates	Provisioning
Encrypt / Decrypt Data	Secure Command and Control
Device Twin	Secure Registration

Device

On Device Data Encryption	In flight Data Encryption
Tamper proof	Secure Cloud Registration
Controller Code	Microprocessor

Chapter 8: The Execution

In this chapter, we will highlight the scope of the MVE.

The MVE experience for the Smart Service should include some components of each of the Disruption Levers.

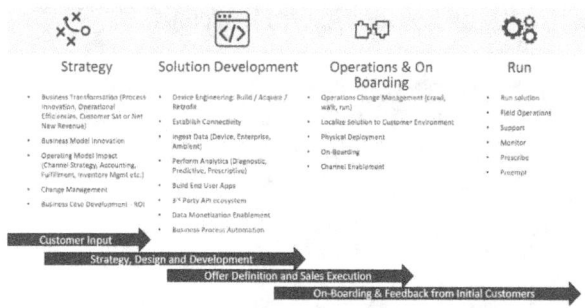

So, everything from your strategy which will include your business model opportunities, your operating model impact and the change management associated with that, your business case development which has your cost investment, must be part of your minimum value product. The customer input that influenced the initial scope has to be part of your minimum value product. Business process automation and solution development, whether it's device engineering on your side, establishing connectivity, ingesting data, performing analytics, or building end-user applications should be part of the scope for the MVE.

Elements of all of these things must come alive on some level, whether it's in the crawl, walk, or run stage, so the end consumer can benefit from and fall in love with your connected solution.

It is important to ensure that the onboarding process of your product or service is easy and well-enabled as part of your customer experience.

Localize the solution to your customer's environment if this an add-on. If it's a physical deployment, ensure there is an ability for your organization or your partners to do so.

Finally, being able to support your customers when your product or service is on the market is an important consideration. Imagine a scenario where your customers get more real-time information from your connected product than your own customer support personnel do. If customers have a problem and they call you, have you enabled your customer service representatives to have meaningful conversations with them? Are your field personnel able to communicate and provide real-time information? Can they prescribe and preempt? Are your people able to cross sell and upsell?

There are a few key foundational areas that impact the successful launch of your Smart

Service. Some of these have been discussed at various points in the book but it is worth summarizing the key aspects of execution that will be required. You want to ensure that the following fundamentals have been accounted for:

- Organization Support – One of the first parts of ensuring success is to extend consensus amongst business groups. The best way to get consensus and program funding is to ensure people sign up for specific goals. If the outcome is increasing organic growth in the number of customers, then you need to make sure you work with operational teams, like marketing and sales, to ensure that they sign up for exact numbers toward organic growth. If the goal is net new revenue or incremental revenue from an existing product or service, you need to work with the appropriate teams, like finance, to ensure that the appropriate people make the appropriate commitments.

- Offer Definition – Riding side-by-side with organization support is the concept of an offer. You need to make sure that once the service or product is on the market, people know about it. The offer could be for them to sign up for it, download it, try it for free for 30 days, etc. There could be an enablement on social channels, so people can extend the virtues of your product or service to others.

- An offer needs to exist, and that stream of work needs to be accounted for by the product management or service management group. You may not be responsible for defining the offer, but it is in your program's best interest that your organization has one.

- Sales Enablement – Sales enablement is at the heart of every organization's ability to create a pipeline of opportunities and enable sellers to successfully sell your product or service. This includes enabling people in the frontline, like client directors, sales professionals, pre-sales individuals, field personnel, customer service managers, distributors, resellers, and other types of partners and channels. These are all people who need to know about your service and need to love your product as much as you do, they can be brand ambassadors and are positioned to effortlessly speak about the value of this new product and service. Enabling them with the right material, case studies, training, etc. needs to be done to ensure success. Your product management organization will be primarily responsible for this stream of work.

- Risk Management – Risk management is an important element of your digital transformation blueprint. Making sure that risks are clearly communicated, how and when those risks are mitigated, and who the owners of those risks are so people are not pointing at each other is an important element of successfully managing risks.

Having a true program manager who focuses on the quick mitigation of risks is an important part of ensuring your team and your extended teams are executing flawlessly.

- Governance – From a program execution standpoint, your success holders—stake holders, executive committees, heads of operations—are impacted by the transformation. All of these individuals need to be part of your steering committee. These are people with whom you are continually and proactively communicating status updates on progress, dependencies, risks, risk mitigation, roadmaps, the customer journey, business model opportunities, and product or service innovation investments. This is to ensure that the consensus you've built continues to be formed throughout your transformation program life cycle.

- Continuous Innovation – Continuous innovation is the idea that once you have that little nugget of success completed and available in the market that your customers can touch and use, you should have the ability to capture and synthesize any questions, feedback, and opinions. This is also analogous to the virtuous cycle concept discussed earlier in the book. In the digital economy, ideas are the cornerstone of your transformation journey, and harnessing those ideas from others in every way possible is important for continually delivering what people want. Continuous innovation is the ability to harness those ideas and rapidly alter and modify your set of priorities by mapping customer feedback in real-time. What is important here is the ability to change your plans and priorities and then communicate that effectively through the various chains of operations. It is important to ensure that you are able to go from one success point to the next with the highest level of impact. Ensuring this process works is the foundation of ensuring that the blueprint is successful.

Chapter 9- Choosing Your Partners

The type of transformation you're undertaking and its complexity will dictate the type of partners you choose. The selection of a partner in this digital economy is about speed and lower risks and costs, more so now than ever before. Because knowledge may have been previously unavailable in this phase, there is a huge amount of strategic consulting available to you. You have to consider whether you are taking your whole organization forward or you are going to experiment. If you are going to experiment, you probably don't have the budget or the luxury to spend millions on strategic consulting. You are probably better off experimenting with niche players and developing your own capability within the organization to lead this phase.

With the advent of the Cloud, there are a few platform services companies out there that are truly leaders in this phase. These organizations offer so many tools, methodologies, and micro-services to build your digital capabilities and portfolio.

Platform and service companies are a key consideration for you. The other key thing is considering management consultancies versus systems integrators (SI) versus platform and service companies. These companies are experiencing their own huge transformation. Moving forward, we'll likely see management consultancy firms buying SIs, SIs trying to turn more management consulting firm, and platform services trying to build their own services capabilities. Our recommendation to you is to consider the hierarchy of the transformation diagram that we talked about earlier in the book, analyzing the complexity of the transformation you are undertaking. We strongly advise you to clearly consider the capabilities you will require to both transition your culture and to build a digital enterprise. Once these capabilities are clear to you, you can then make an informed decision about which partners you need at the various points within your digital journey. We would also be happy for you to contact us, so we can advise you on how to structure your partnerships.

If you're configuring the Internet of Things, let's consider what is commodity and what is a rare skill. SIs are typically a commodity because you are trying to piece together different technology components and integrate these systems. Bridging the divide between hardware design, cloud and software as we discussed in the last chapter, is a rare skill, and there are fewer companies that have both the hardware engineering skills and the software and Cloud skills to deliver the connected product and the smart service. But, you can have a partner like a

Systems Integrator take on the risk and bring on a hardware engineering partner under the project umbrella in effect taking on the risk for delivering the end to end solution.

If you're looking at a large-scale transformation with a lot of legacy, then you'll probably want to consider one of the large SIs or management consultancies, or maybe you'll have outsourcers come in and support you. However, if your transformation is going completely to Cloud, and you have very little legacy integration that needs to be done, then you know working with a PaaS partner is probably best. In conclusion, if you're going to have a huge amount of legacy, work with an SI. If you're getting rid of most of your legacy, then lead with your Cloud platform company.

If you're considering a customer experience transformation, there are SaaS companies that are built as cloud businesses on customer transformation and customer centric engagement strategies. If it's about OPEX reduction, then we would direct you toward the traditional SIs.

When you're considering your partnerships, think about the DNA of your own organization. How much do you like to insource versus outsource work? Some of this could have to do with the highly regulated environment you might be in. Finally, consider the skills gap. This applies to the executives, managers, business people, and IT people. In this digital economy, skills are scarce.

Choosing partners in balance with building your own internal capabilities is paramount.

Summary

In this book, we've attempted to give you a practitioner's guide to help you navigate and chart a course through this increasingly complex world of digital disruption. You will have recognized that the stakes are very high, and the success rate of organizations tends to be low, with very few examples of good success in each vertical.

In this age, it is a very big gamble, both in achieving the outcome you're trying to drive and meeting it in time to benefit from the first mover advantage as well as the huge risk to the return on investment of this particular transformation.

The other gamble involved is a cultural one. You have a legacy business, and you're trying not to distract the core business with this new experiment based, innovative start. How will you keep your legacy and your existing cash cow, delivering your profits? How will you keep the people associated with that cash cow feeling motivated and not sidelined because of all the interesting, creative startups being implemented by transformation teams?

We've talked about how to build digital momentum and take the organization with you, creating a leadership position for yourself as the self-proclaimed digital leader. Hopefully, you will have recognized that there are huge amounts of complexities driven from the collisions hardware engineering, software engineering, the Cloud, your internal operations, your business model and your go-to-market model and sales motion.

Unless it is driven with a structured model, as we have put forward, the transformation could become quite chaotic and costly. We recognize that leaders and organizational structures change, so how can you stay true to the original outcome that the digital transformation was meant to achieve amongst all of the other changes that may be going on within your organization?

We have shared several key frameworks with you, and we've also shared how-to's, but this is just the tip of the iceberg. As anybody who has been through any of these digital transformations knows, there is a huge amount of both complexity and emotion in terms of the people involved That emotion associated with these types of transformations can be positive or negative.

As thought-leaders and practitioners in the field of digital disruption and smart services, we would be delighted to work with you. We have established a website to support this book. You can find it at www.digitalgamble.com. We encourage you to visit our website for more information and for the frameworks that we have referred to in this book. You can also contact us at winning@digitalgamble.com

The era of this fourth industrial revolution, is going to see companies, including huge brands, going out of business while new huge companies and brands are created. The rates at which companies go out of business will equal the rate at which new ones are created. Whether you are the enterprise, a partner or an employee, we see this as a tremendous opportunity for creating new business opportunities or personal career growth, whilst you traverse this digital journey.